A guidebook shouldn't really need instructions but for the avoidance of confusion that you head out on to the heath with this book poking from your pocket, find a bench sit and then digest the accompanying blurb from the perspective of the bench, perhaps trotting round the locale to check on nearby points of interest.

Hampstead Heath has long been associated with literary types so there's a loose poetic theme to each of the top ten along with a big scale map to save you from inappropriate diversions. If you're really lost, check the main map at the back which features all the benches plus some reserves for further deliberation. There's also a suggestion on what to do if you think our top ten is misguided. Similarly, while we've done everything we possibly can (be arsed to do) to check on the veracity of the information relating to the environs of each bench, if you think you know better then feel free to Instagram us as specified at the back.

Almost all of Hampstead Heath's benches are dedicated to someone or other, usually posthumously. Indeed several of the more secluded ones are suitable venues on which to reminisce your own dearest departed, or perhaps ponder some indulgent existential crisis. So it is in the spirit of free expression that we invite you, the reader, to dedicate this book to anyone who's wandered lonely as a cloud, eluding London's madding crowd.

Dedicated to:

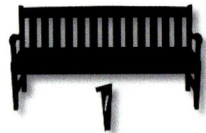

A Green Thought

In Memory of Barbara Myers 1927-1987

The words of Andrew Marvell seem written for this very spot. Visit on a quiet summer's afternoon when bright green duckweed covers the Iron Pan ponds and let your mind drift back to 1680 when Mr Marvell wrote *The Garden*.

Annihilating all that's made

to a green thought in a green shade

Marvell had a cottage on Highgate Hill, though back then the heath was far less woody and much more heath-like. In his day Sandy Heath was level with Spaniard's road. Over the years its bagshot sand with its heavy iron content was carted off to foundaries and building sites, creating the gulleys that now double as a mountain bike playground, especially to your right. Over to your left you will see a couple of ancient oaks planted in Marvell's time. What remains of their root mound has been fenced by a raised ring of logs. A sign explains how they were saved after removal of the surrounding sand left them high and dry.

The path behind you leads to Spaniard's Inn with its London toll booth across the

Two Tree Hill's ancient oaks in the morning mist

The Spaniard's - haunt of Dick Turpin & Dracula?

narrow road. Named after the Spanish Ambassador to James I and dating from 1585, the pub has a rich history and is mentioned in both Charles Dicken's *The Pickwick Papers* and Bram Stoker's *Dracula*.

Legend has it that this was the haunt of Dick Turpin, whose father switched from butcher to pub landlord. Though Spaniards Road seems the perfect spot to shout *stand and deliver!*, and coaches were indeed ambushed as they headed towards the toll gate, Turpin was in reality more Essex lad than swashbuckling highwayman, his story like so many others romanticised over time.

If you continue on the path towards Golders Hill Park and the Old Bull & Bush, take the first right just after you exit Sandy Heath and snoop along Wildwood Terrace all the way down to Wildwood Road. Turn left, and left again into Hampstead Way and soon on the right search for a white blockhouse behind a fence that is the entrance to North End tube station. Its construction was abondoned in 1906 following reassessment of local demand. It lay vacant until the 1950s when a 197 step staircase was installed to give access to a floodgate control room in the abandoned station below. It was intended to become operational in the event of a nuclear attack, so it might see some action yet.

If you find the presence of people along the adjacent path too much to bear, then head past the ancient oaks of two tree hill, towards Whitestone Pond, where you'll discover more secluded benches on which to indulge a green thought in a green shade.

Tube staircase installation 1956

Sweep up the Wood

There are two moveable benches in the copse, this one offers a glimpse of Kenwood House through the trees

Here you sit under a lovely old fir tree, one amongst a copse of four, offering glimpses of Kenwood through the trees, and the renovated but under-utilised Dairy in the distance. The bench is not fixed to the ground and does tend to move, as does the extent of the undergrowth and therefore view. The dates carved in the dedication to Nasser Kalantery, 1957-2007, mark an early death. It's a quiet, contemplative spot, the evergreen firs recalling a graveyard's yews.

Pour away the ocean and sweep up the wood;

For nothing now can ever come to any good.

The final two lines of W. H. Auden's Funeral Blues, though somewhat hackneyed thanks to Four Weddings and a Funeral, still pack a heart-wrenching emotional punch. In the film the poem is read at the funeral of a gay lover. Auden was also gay, and back in 1938 it's easy to assume he wrote it in the depths of grief about some secret affair. In fact the poem was originally conceived as a send-up of all too public outpourings of grief. Wystan Hugh Auden wrote the poem's first two stanzas for a play entitled *The Ascent of F6*. A mountaineer, desperate to pip a rival nation and claim the fictional F6 for king and country, is rather too hasty and dies in the process. Auden added the final two stanzas some years later and turned parody into poignancy.

If you continue eastward you enter the enclosure of South Wood. Turn left and then stick right and you will soon ascend to the dueling ground. There were several popular spots around London to indulge in pistols at dawn, and this small clearing deep in the woods was one of them; big enough to fit the 10-20 paces typically agreed upon, and convenient enough for a swift exit out of town should the contest result in a fatality. Despite the fact that a dueling fatality was adjudged murder, court enforcement was lax. Indeed in 1814 a British army officer was court-marshalled and cashiered for failing to issue a challenge when publicly insulted.

The dueling ground circa 1945

The aristocratic etiquette of the duel was formally prescribed in the Irish Code of 1777. A list of its 26 commandments might be kept for reference by a gentleman in his pistol case, should a dispute arise about how to settle the dispute.

There are usually two benches to be found beneath the fir trees. The one with its back to the copse, and fittingly its back to the any passers-by, seems the more appropriate spot to seek solace.

The entrance to the dueling ground as it looks today

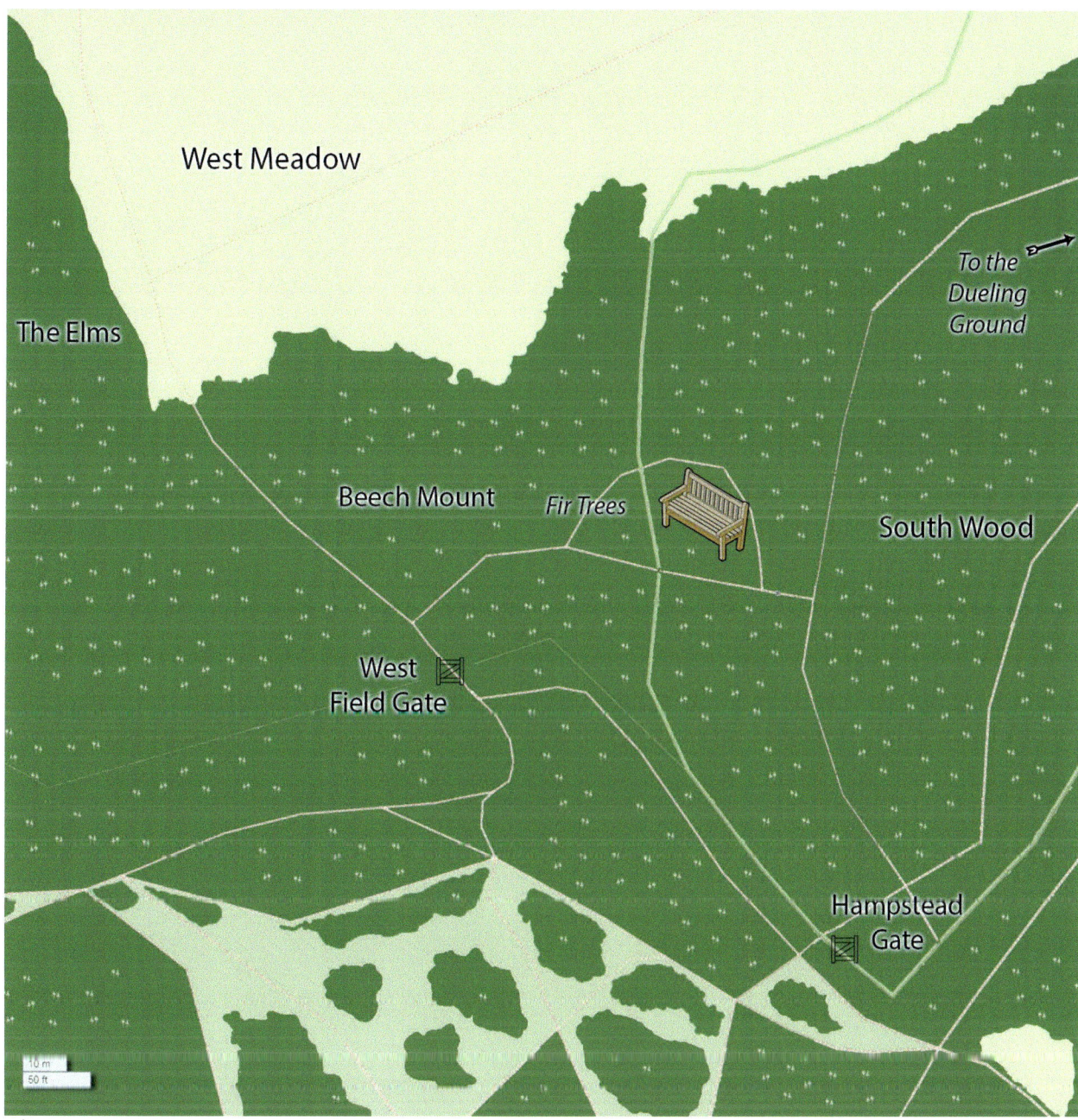

Famous Bigshots

Here you sit in the Heath anomaly that is Athlone House Garden, a stone's throw from the gardens of famous bigshots. As Caroline Knox eloquently put it

…snooded consorts,
fiscal eggheads and erstwhile tightwads

Behind you are the 11 acres of Beechwood House, former residence of the King of Saudi Arabia, the Emir of Qatar, and current owner, big yacht record-holder, former 30% Arsenal owner and now Everton investor, and all round nice guy, Alisher Usmanov. Ali served six years for fraud back in the USSR, though that blemish has since been expunged. Following the collapse of the Soviet Union he made billions in metal, mining and media. He married a rhythmic gymnastics coach, and she introduced Vlad the Putin to another rhythmic gymnast Alina Kabaeva.

This was good news for Usmanov. Soon Putin, a mere 30 years Kabaeva's senior, fell for her flexible charms; holding as she does, the title 'Honoured Master of Sports'. She has already had, reportedly, two children with Putin and is expecting a third in 2022, though no one likes to talk about it for obvious reasons.

Usmanov bought Beechwood for just under £50 million in the late noughties. Following the invasion of Ukraine the Tories finally got round to implementing sanctions that should really

Beechwood's back garden

have been enforced years ago. Of course by this time Usmanov had already switched his £170 million UK property empire into an irrevocable trust and removed himself as a beneficiary, leaving his family conservators of the filched billions.

The gated grounds of Athlone House are to your right and boast a similarly colourful history. It ran MI6 training courses during the war under the guise of an RAF convalescent home. The NHS used it as a home for people with dementia, but sadly it seems to have been forgotten about and was left derelict in 2003.

Developers reared their ugly heads and were granted permission to build the 22 luxury apartments of Kenwood Place, on condition of refurbishing the main house and donating a strip of woodland to the public, Athlone House Garden. Naturally, the developers decided to play the long game and let the main house rot. The Kharafis of Kuwait bought it in 2006 expecting their billions could bulldoze the preservation order. However thanks to the Highgate Society's 5,000 strong petition, and some principled Camden councillors, they repeatedly failed.

The bench that backs on to Beechwood

Another Russian oligarch Mikhail Fridman, also recently sanctioned, paid around £65 million for Athlone House in 2016, and now, finally, refurbishment of its iconic square tower is complete.

The shack that sank the developers

In one corner of Athlone's grounds lived Harry 'the hermit' Hallowes, a well-loved Irish tramp, who counted Python and Highgate resident Terry Gilliam among his friends. After being evicted from his council flat in 1985, he built a homemade shack in the derelict grounds and squatted for 22 years. Ironically during the developer's attempts to evict him he was granted ownership of his little corner plot. The film *Hampstead* starring Diane Keaton and Brendan Gleeson loosely tells the story. He's long gone now, but please salute him with a finger up to the bigshots.

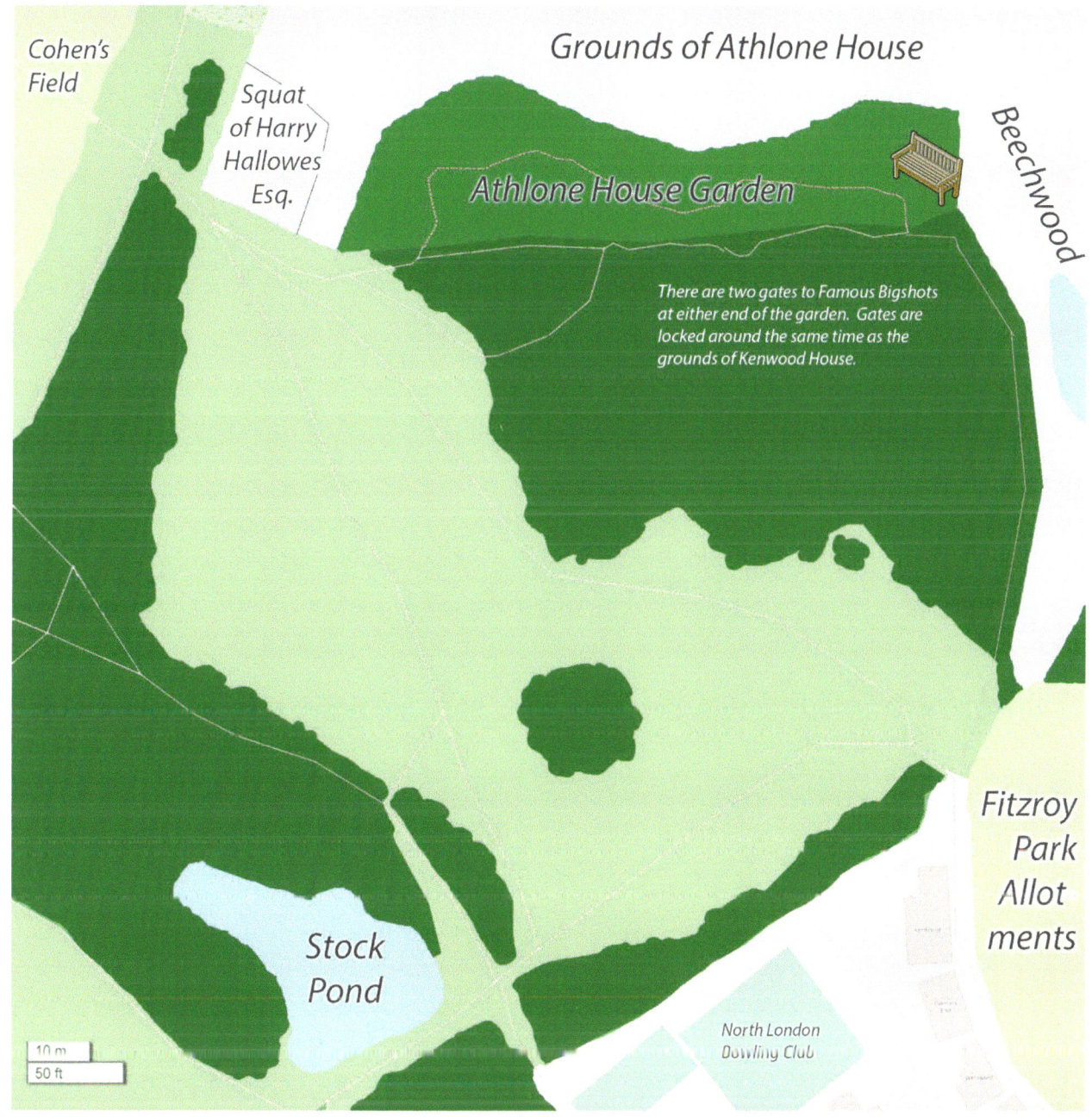

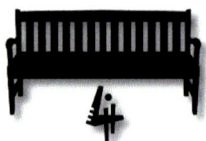

Health Fanatic

While one admires the righteous dedication of the keep fit set, their proliferation does make it increasingly hard to suppress a Tourette like compulsion to yell *Jogger!* each time an off-duty financial vunderkind pants past; particularly if sporting PwC, JP Morgan, or similar shameful corporate insignia. To quote the legendary John Cooper Clarke:

"He's a Health Fanatic... He makes you sick"

Paul Ross on an icy blue winter's day

That rant shoehorns us awkwardly into this bench overlooking Vale of Health Pond. There's a couple of benches to choose from, but the winner is dedicated to *Paul Ross*.

The name Vale of Health, first recorded in 1801, was intended to divert from the fact it was originally a stagnant malarial marsh known as Gangmoor. In the early 18th century it became Hatchett's Bottom, after Samuel Hatch, a harness maker and local cottager. In 1777 the Hampstead Water Company drained the bog and created the pond you see before you, framed by the sweeping back gardens of the well-heeled. By 1821 local residents were petitioning for the removal of the *poor houses*, a tentative first step towards building the *Vale of Wealth* you see today.

One of the vale's first residents was the essayist Leigh Hunt who hosted regular get-togethers in the early 19th century with Shelley, Keats, Byron and other literary illuminati. John Keats lived in lodgings on the other side of East Heath Road at 1 Well Walk, along with his two younger brothers. He made great friends with Charles Armitage Brown who lived in Wentworth Place, now Keats House Museum, and it was here where he met and fell in love with the girl next door, Francis Brawne, inspiring his *Ode to Fanny* in 1819.

Following the opening of Hampstead Junction Railway in 1860, the heath became accessible to the hoi polloi. Several fairs sprung up to cater for lairy cockneys who descended in their bank holiday droves. The song *Appy Ampstead!* by music hall comedian Albert Chevalier brought the heath national notoriety. On Easter Monday 1910 crowds peaked at an estimated 200,000. Local showman Harry Cox exhibited his *Vale of Health Perpetual Pleasure Fair*, with boat rides on the pond, steam roundabouts, shies, and nearby, everything from pony rides to peepshows.

The Vale of Health Hotel and a Perpetual Pleasure Fair once stood where Spencer House now prevails

The Vale of Health Hotel, built in 1863, hosted the politically assiduous Athenaeum Club, boasting over a thousand mostly German members. Ironically during World War I it became a factory dedicated to their annihilation. A few doors up there is a plaque commemorating the poet and writer D.H. Lawrence who lived there in 1915 with his German wife Freida. They were walking home across the Heath late that summer when they spotted her countrymen in a Zeppelin overhead, conducting one of the first air-raids of the Great War.

The caravan park of yesteryear with a trailer for dodgem cars in the foreground behind the fence

The hotel also contained artists' studios. Sir Stanley Spencer painted here from 1914 to 1927. Sadly the hotel fell into dereliction and was demolished in 1964 to make way for Spencer House, the six story block of flats facing you across the pond from the bench.

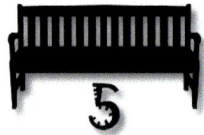

Mansions Built by Nature's Hand

So wrote Heath regular William Wordsworth referring to the stars, (which you can view from the nearby Hampstead Scientific Society Observatory, a wonderfully eccentric enterprise perched atop a reservoir and open to the public on clear weekend nights). Wordsworth's poem equally befits the Pergola, its overgrown vines and exotic flowers creating a mansion built by nature's hand. It offers several choice spots to relax, though being a licensed wedding venue, avoid the weekends when it can be infested by nuptial photo shoots.

Now she walks through her sunken dreams to the seat with the clearest view, a.k.a. bench five

The Pergola is a legacy of Lord Leverhulme, who moved into *The Hill* manor house now *Inverforth House* in 1904. It was completed in 1906 by renowned landscape architect Thomas Mawson to host extravagant Edwardian garden parties. It has since been considerably extended, the far end offering views north-west to Harrow on the Hill. The Hill Garden was laid out by Leslie Mansfield in the 1920s and was first opened to the public along with the Pergola in 1963. Inverforth House was converted into two houses and seven apartments in the 1990s, having served as the

Orthopaedic Society Hospital since the late 50s, by which time the pergola had fallen into disrepair.

There are several lovely benches tucked away in the Hill Garden's walls, but the prime spot is dedicated to Tom Bailie and looks down on the beautiful landscaped garden below.

A little up from the Pergola on the highest spot in metropolitan London sits Jack Straw's Castle, named after one of the three leaders of the Peasants' Revolt of 1381. A pub has stood here since the early 18th century and was a favoured haunt of Charles Dickins and Karl Marx. Like the Spaniard's it features in Dracula, Van Helsing taking supper there before vampire hunting on the heath. The original bay window in the shot below was possibly blown out during the Zeppelin raid of September 1915. The Hampstead War Memorial stands opposite the pub. It was unveiled in 1922 but didn't deter the Germans from returning to blitz the pub and adjacent Castle Hotel in 1941.

Top spot in the Hill Garden, Tom Bailie 1908-1981

Jack Straw's Castle and hotel shortly before the Great War

The present day Jack Straw's castle was reincarnated as a monolithic wooden block in 1964 by Raymond Erith. The poet laureate Sir John Betjeman described it as *a delight* and *true Middlesex*, but some feel it lost its charm, ever more so since conversion from pub to apartments in 2002.

The Observatory as seen by the stars

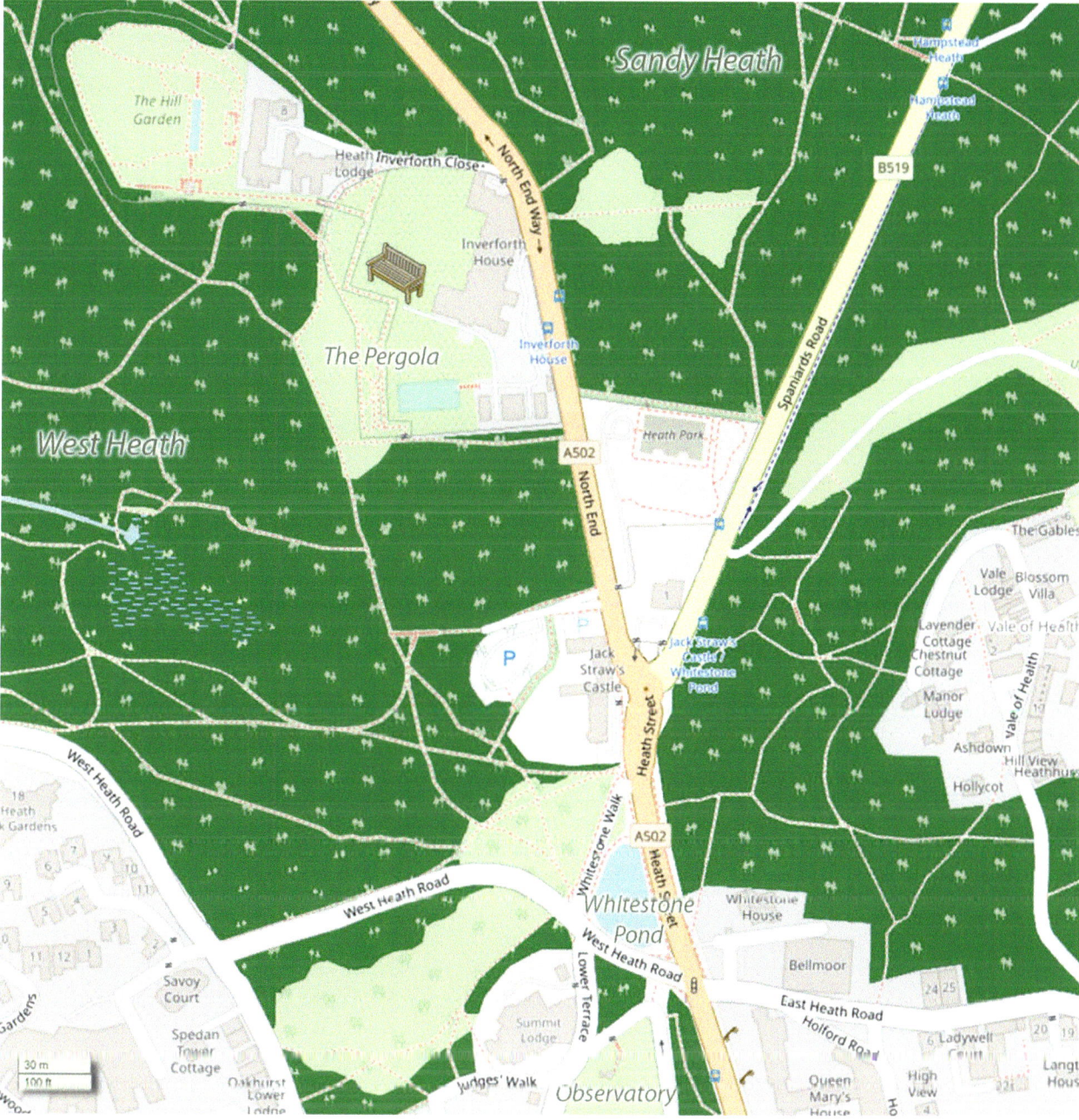

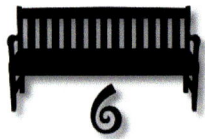

A Thing of Beauty

Almost in the middle of the Heath is the funerary monument known as Boudica's Mound. Historic England added it to their National Heritage List of protected monuments in 1965, calling it Boadicea's Grave. That spelling bows to the Romans, so I'm going with a derivation from *bouda*, Celtic for victory. Essex lads of the time would have pronounced it bow-dee-kah, whereas today's residents would just say Victoria, or Vicky for short.

The tumulus was first noted on Stukeley's map of 1725

The Order of Bards, Ovates and Druids placed a wreath on the mound during the solstice of 1967. Boudica, the druids explained, was cremated hence the lack of a body found in the mound when archeologist Charles Hercules Read conducted extensive excavations in 1894. It's more likely to be an ancient Bronze Age bell barrow, and nothing to do with the Queen of the Iceni who led the revolt against the Romans, burning Londinium to the ground while General Suetonius was away, circa 60 CE. Suetonius wrote of Boudica *"In stature she was very tall, in appearance most terrifying, in the glance of her eye most fierce, with a tawny mass of hair that fell to her hips"*. No doubt we'd all look a bit narked having been ransacked, flogged and our daughters raped. For a more contemporary depiction we have Thomas Thornycroft's bronze of 1902, *Boadicea and her Daughters*. She stands astride a huge chariot charging vengefully towards the Houses of Parliament.

A bronzed Boudica and daughters

Several benches surround the mound. Our top pick is inscribed with the first line of William Keats *Endymion "A thing of beauty is a joy forever"*, and the view is certainly a joy. The bench to the left actually has a better view but it's dedication to a *"People's Poet & Hanging Magistrate"* is less poetic.

The city peeps over the treeline

Another Keats classic, *Ode to a Nightingale,* is said to have been inspired by the chirping of a bird he'd heard while sitting in the garden of nearby Spaniard's Inn. He popped back to Wentworth Place, now a museum, and promptly penned said ode.

Keats House is now a museum

Around this time Millfield Lane on the Highgate side of the Heath became known as Poets' Lane. According to poet and editor of *The Examiner,* James Leigh Hunt, it was *"an appellation it richly deserves"*. Keats, Coleridge, Byron and Shelley were among *Hunt's Circle*, and though Keats met Coleridge just once, on Poet's Lane, he wrote that they had *"broached a thousand things"* as they rambled round Boadicea's mound. Coleridge was less effusive in his recollection of their meeting, though to be fair he was trying to kick a sizeable opium addiction at the time.

Down the hill to your left is the model boating pond ruined, according to enthusiasts, by the flood defence revamp circa 2015 which rendered it too shallow for sail boats' deep keels. Likewise the adjacent men's bathing pond is no longer a hot spot for cruising. Things have moved on since George Michael famously quipped: *"It's a much nicer place to get some quick and honest sex than standing in a bar E'd off your tits"*. These days the entrance to the men's pond is just a nice sunbathing spot; but don't despair, fans of vintage cottaging can still be found in the woods behind Jack Straw's Castle.

Sun worshippers outside the men's pond in its heyday

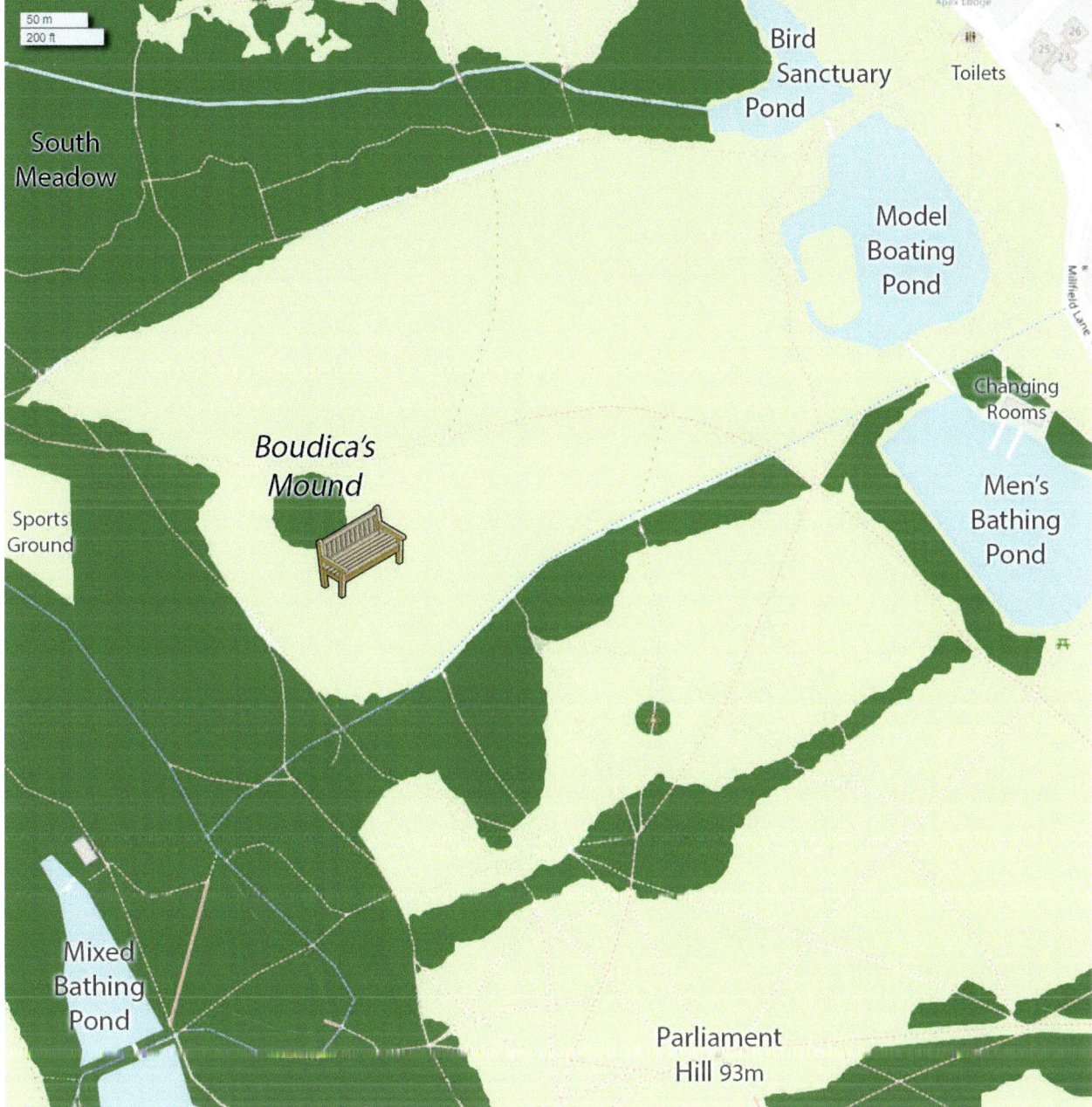

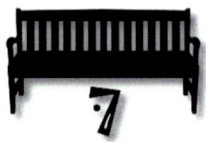

Teacher & Hitchhiker

South Meadow has several lovely benches dotted around the grassy paths that head down to the gully. It's a wonderful spot to lie prostrate in the long yellowed grass, transfixed by the electric blue yonder and the swaying treetops floating above. One of the best benches, dedicated to Margaret & Hunter, appears between four silver birches framing it with a V-sign, but for a bit more privacy head down the gully and walk back uphill again. A clearing appears and you'll find an ancient oak with a bench facing downhill. The intriguing but incorrectly hyphenated inscription reads *In Loving Memory of Susi Holzer Teacher and Hitch-hiker*. The epitaph conjures thoughts of a wandering free spirit, rather like Britain's most poetic wanderer the late laureate William Wordsworth. His most famous line could hardly be more aposite for a man who was said to wander ten miles or more each day in his native lake district.

Margaret & Hunter by the V of four silver birch trees

Teacher & Hitchhiker by the old oak tree

> *I wandered lonely as a cloud*
> > *that floats on high o'er vales and hills*

His poem *London from Hampstead Heath* betrays the fact he was also a regular visitor to the heath and friends with the neighbourhood's many romantic poets.

Viaduct Bridge circa 1910

Should you continue up the hill past the sports ground on your left and then turn right you soon arrive at Viaduct Bridge, or Wilson's Folly after the graspingly rapacious Thomas Maryon Wilson. Having inherited most of the east side of the heath at the age of 20, our precocious developer planned to bolster his fortune by creating East Park Estate. A drive was to be lined with 28 villas styled on those that surround Regent's Park, each set in two acres of gardens, with the whole development surrounded by a park of exotic trees. The bridge formed a grand entrance to the estate with an ornamental pool created below. In 1845 a foundation stone was laid to much ceremony, but alas the viaduct's foundations collapsed several times during construction draining Wilson's rapidly thinning reserves of capital. His plans were further thwarted by disapproving and influential neighbours. Lord Mansfield of Kenwood and the founders of the National Trust, among others, ensured that Bird Bridge and Viaduct Bridge are all that remain today.

Viaduct bridge as seen from Bird Bridge

Just beyond the eastern edge of South Meadow, by an old fallen, tree you can sit on *A Great Time* and gaze across the open field to the spire of St Michael's church poking over the tree tops. Witanhurst, the capital's largest private residence after Buckingham Palace, is adjacent. It's huge walnut panelled ballroom was once the setting for BBC's Fame Academy, a forerunner of X Factor et al. It is currently in the clutches of Putin crony Andry Guryev, who bought it off the Assad family via a property developer. Guryev spent years annoying the neighbours by digging out two basement floors that span the entire mansion's footprint. At present the only consolation is that he's sanctioned, banished to the indignity of living with his countrymen.

Another oligarch's gilded cage leers over the tree tops

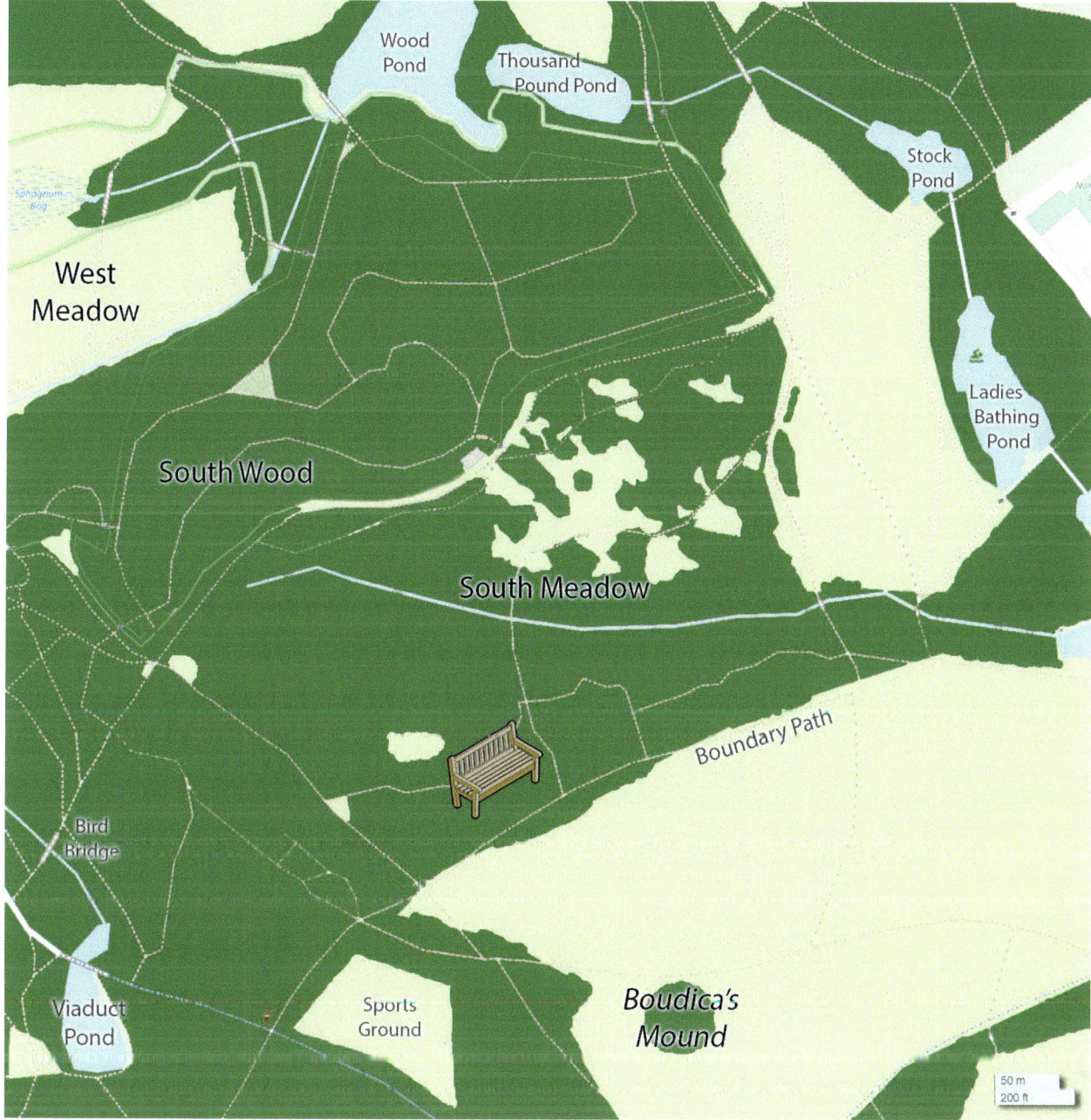

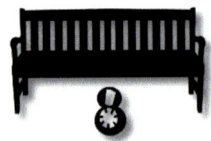

A Masterpiece

The bench is straight ahead nestled in the far corner

On a late summer's evening, gazing across the windblown sunburnt grass of West Meadow, while the sun sets on the horizon, is one of the Heath's masterpieces. To reach it you may have trotted past a Reclining Figure by Henry Moore or Barbara Hepworth's Monolith. The artists were Belsize Park neighbours and very much part of the 1930s Hampstead Modernist set. You may even have snuck a peek at one of the world's most priceless masterpieces, Rembrandt's *Self Portrait with Two Circles*. He painted 80 odd self-portraits, and this is among the best, housed in the ostensibly lax security of Kenwood House.

> *Self-portraits understand, and old age can divest,*
> *With truthful changes, us of fear of death.*

These lines from the poem *Rembrandt's Late Self-Portraits* were written by Elizabeth Jennings in 1975. When Rembrandt completed a self-portrait, he would be confronted with his inner psyche's appraisal of himself, leading to a deeper understanding of the world

Self-Portrait with Two Circles 1665–69, Kenwood House

and his place within it; just as old age, and the truthful examination of one's aging appearance, can divest us of fear of death.

Which segues us seemlessly from sham analysis to *Sham Bridge*. This grade II listed trompe l'oeil is attributed to Robert Adams and was built circa 1781 to enhance the view from Kenwood . You can just see it from the bench by the Henry Moore, or trot down the hill for a sneak look behind the scenes.

Sham Bridge in the distance behind the Henry Moore

Hampstead Heath's association with subterfuge does not end with the Sham Bridge. The spy turned author John le Carré had a favourite bench where he would write, "*tucked under a spreading tree and set apart from its companions*". The Mixed Ponds were the backdrop for *Tinker, Tailor, Soldier, Spy* staring Gary Oldman; and in *Smiley's People* General Vladimir is murdered on Lime Avenue, a gravel track leading into the heath from the late author's house in Gainsborough Gardens. Smiley discovers a cigarette packet with a roll of film lodged in a tree to solve the murder, but the bench Le Carré himself favoured remains a mystery.

This bench dedicated to Melvin Bragg's wife is prime suspect for Le Carré's mystery bench

There are several benches in the pasture ground beneath Kenwood House that are almost as appealing as West Meadow's bench eight, but when a big empty sky looms overhead (as seen overleaf), this spot could be anywhere; certainly not a mere four miles from Piccadilly Circus.

Behind the scenes at the Sham Bridge

Morning's Minion

"I caught this morning, morning's minion,

kingdom of daylight's dauphin, dapple-dawn-drawn Falcon"

So wrote Gerard Manley Hopkins with a flourish of hyphens. Dedicated to Jesus Christ Almighty, *The Windhover* is an 1877 love poem to the wonder of nature, specifically a hovering falcon.

Can yan spot all 22 birdies carved into the log?

No doubt Kate Springett, official bird recorder for the Heath, founding president of the Marylebone Birdwatching Society, founder of the Springett Fund for bird-related beneficence and twitcher extraordinaire, was familiar with the morning's minion; and you might contemplate their tweets in this quiet protected corner of the heath, its two acres dedicated to her shortly before her death in 1995.

Bench number nine is actually a log. There are two gates to Springett's Wood a few yards apart. Near the top gate you will find this commemorative seat, bearing the inscription *Kate Springett Birdwatcher 1906-95*. It was beautifully carved by Kate Pyper from a nearby fallen oak in 2005 but is now sadly showing its age. Try and find all 22 birds, among them tit and thrush, but no game cock, dickcissel, imperial shag or even manly falcon.

A Sea of Springett Ivy

A 1945 caricature of jolly old hockey stick Dr C.E.M. Joad

Adjacent to Springett's Wood is *Dr Joad's Hockey Pitch,* and behind you looms a radio mast that is not quite ancient enough to have broadcast the BBC's hugely popular panel show of the 40s and 50s: *The Brain's Trust.* One of its stars was celebrity philosopher Dr Cyril Joad, who attempted to answer questions that might befuddle the ordinary mortal. This sloping field earnt its monicker from the regular Sunday knockabouts Cyril would enjoy with other jolly hockey sticks.

He was a controversial figure who entertained several Mrs Joads in his nearby Hampstead home. He famously described sexual desire as *"a buzzing bluebottle that needs to be swatted promptly before it distracts a man of intellect from higher things"*.

Inevitably his bombast blew him into blunder. After publicly boasting that he cheated the railways whenever he could, he was caught without a ticket and duly prosecuted. This hoo-ha led to a sacking by the BBC, and a slow drift into ignominy.

If you continue on through Dr Joad's Hockey Pitch the next open space you reach is the Upper Fairground, site of bank holiday entertainments for generations. Just below on the edge of the Vale of Health is the curious temporary caravan park owned by the Abbott fairground dynasty. They have occupied this temporary site for well over a century, indeed Violet *Hampstead* Miller lived here all her life and lasted till over 100. Funfair paraphernalia would often be parked up, though less so in recent years as the fair's demise seems an inevitability.

Predictably, developers have tried to reclassify the showpeople's site as a permanent residence, but being Metropolitan Open Land, and having the wrath of the Heath & Hampstead Society to contend with, their efforts have so far been thwarted.

The last Easter Fair on the Upper Fairground in 2019

Parliament Hill Fields

The view from Parliament Hill is undoubtedly one of the best in London. Two hundred years ago William Wordsworth headed up here to lament the demise of fellow poet and rambler George Crabbe:

Our haughty life is crowned with darkness, Like London with its own black wreath,
On which with thee, O Crabbe! forth-looking, I gazed from Hampstead's breezy heath.

Mayor Johnson's legacy - a shapeless, bloated monstrosity takes centre stage

Today you will see the lofty spires of the Cheese Grater, Gherkin, Heron, Shard, Walkie Talkie, Boomerang and Scalpel; not forgetting the offensively large and dull 22, and of course 42. Canary Wharf's skyscrapers are to the left of the city, with the former Post Office Tower framing the view to the right. It's a dramatically different view to that of a mere decade ago. During his time as Mayor, Johnson rubber-stamped around 400 towers over twenty stories high, and the jury is still out on whether the skyline has changed for the better.

At 98m Parliament Hill is not the highest point in London. Ignoring Bromley, Croydon, Harrow and other burbs, the highest accolade goes to the flagstaff by Whitestone Pond near Jack Straw's Castle at 137m.

A dramatically different skyline in 2011

At the summit of Parliament Hill there are several benches to choose from, but the trees do tend to block out a large chunk of the cityscape and it's always crowded. For a more expansive view, particularly at night, walk down the muddy steps directly ahead till you cross the path below. Turn left and sit on the second bench dedicated to the Remfry family. It instructs you to *"Rest a While on the Heath"*. To steal from Sir John Betjeman's poem *Parliament Hill Fields*:

Sunset on Parliament Hill - a rare selection of empty benches

when the feet are hot and tired…stop here if required

Betjemen may be more famous for his thoughts on bombing Slough, but *Parliament Hill Fields* recalls a boyhood tram ride between Kentish Town and Highgate, and is indebted to this view from the Hill. He started life at the bottom in Parliament Hill Mansions but moved *"Up the hill where stucco houses in Virginia creeper drown"* to 31 Highgate West Hill when still a young boy. The poem references the familiar overground trains rumbling behind the athletics track, the bandstand and Highgate ponds, but also hints at his fascination and fear of the poverty in nearby Kentish Town. In his autobiographical blank verse *Summoned By Bells*, he lies in his bedroom and contemplates life at the bottom of the hill *"Here from my eyrie, as the sun went down, I heard the old North London puff and shunt, glad that I did not live in Gospel Oak."*

Sir John Betjeman departing St Pancras

The imbalance of wealth hasn't changed much over the intervening years, though today the Poet Laureate holds on to his hat in St Pancras station. He looks towards an imagined departure board but sees only the curved station roof, just about visible from the bench if you look for the station's clock tower.

Acknowledgements & Thanks

A huge thank you to Laura Nolte whose kindness and generosity in granting permission to use her beautiful photographs of the heath has really put the icing on the cake, (www.http://blog.lauranolte.com). I would also like to thank Laura Price for permission to use her artfully atmospheric painting of Parliament Hill, Winter Sky, and Joe Melia of the Bristol Short Story Prize for being him.

Other kind souls worth a mention are Jacob Surland and his amazing onefootinrealitygallery.com, Harry Brown, Debra Hurford-Brown, Tim Holmes, Jim Brightwell, David Humphries of the Corporation of London, the London Transport Museum collection, and all the generous people who post their photos for use in the public domain.

Front cover, Winter Bench on Page 3 & Reserves on the bench Page 46: © Laura Nolte
Back Page: The Writer, Giancarlo Neri © Andy Aldridge CC BY 2.0
All photos © Pete Franklyn unless otherwise stated.

Parliament Hill Fields
John Betjeman statue: Edwardx CC BY-SA 3.0
Skyline in 2011: Duncan H CC BY 2.0
Skyline in 2022: PF
Benches at Sunset: © Laura Nolte

Full page painting: Parliament Hill, Winter Sky
© Laura Price https://www.lauralondonart.com/paintings

Teacher & Hitchhiker
South Meadow Margaret & Hunter: © Laura Nolte
Viaduct Bridge from an aeroplane: public domain
Viaduct Bridge from Bird Bridge: © Laura Nolte
Wittenhurst: PF

Full page photo Viaduct Bridge: © Laura Nolte

Morning's Minion
Close up on Kate Springett log:
© Jeff Higley http://www.jeffspace.org/
Springett Ivy: PF
Dr Joad Griff Courier magazine caricature: public domain
Upper Fairground: © Tim Holmes

Full page photo Springett's Wood: PF

A Thing of Beauty
Boudica Tumulus with clouds: © Marc Zakian/Alamy
Boudica Statue: Jason Halsall CC BY-SA 3.0
Bench with view of city over treeline: PF
Keats House Museum: PF
Outside Men's Pond: © Intermore.com

Full page photo of Tumulus: PF

A Masterpiece
West Meadow entrance near Beech Mount: PF
Rembrandt Self Portrait with Two Circles: public domain
Henry Moore with Sham Bridge behind: PF
John Le Carré mystery bench: PF

Full page photo of West Meadow from Bench: PF

Mansions Built by Nature's Hand
Bench with Purple Flowers, Pergola Roses, Hill House Garden Bench: © Laura Nolte
Jack Straw's Castle: public domain
Hampstead Observatory: © Jim Brightwell

Full page photo of the Pergola: Laura Nolte

Health Fanatic

Bench in Snow: © Laura Nolte
Vale of Health Hotel across pond: public domain
Hotel with dodgems wagon: © alondoninheretance.com
Full page photo across Vale of Health Pond: PF

For original map data, a mighty acknowledgement to the magnanimous Open Street Map and all its contributors: https://www.openstreetmap.org/ licenced under the Open Data Commons Open Database License (ODbL).

And finally a big kiss to the wonderful Pascale for sage advice and always being right xxx

Famous Bigshots

Beechwood: © The Village
Bench: PF
Harry Hallowes: © Shutterstock
Full page photo of Athlone House: PF

Sweep up the Wood

Bench under fir tree: PF
Duelling Ground 1945: © Eric Hosking
Duelling Ground 2022: PF
Full page photo from Beech Mount: © Laura Nolte

A Green Thought

Barbara Myers bench: PF
Oak trees in mist: © David Humphries, Corporation of London
The Spaniard's Inn: © Jacob Surland https://onefootinrealitygallery.com/
North End tube: ©TfL from the London Transport Museum collection
Full page photo of Iron Pan Pond: © Corp. of London

Links to creative commons licences: https://creativecommons.org/licenses/by/2.0/deed.en
https://creativecommons.org/licenses/by-sa/3.0/deed.en

Reserves on the bench

The main map has ten more reserves to make a top 20. You might want to try them all for size and assess them for vista. The choices will inevitably court controversy so it might be worth mentioning seclusion was high on our criteria. No doubt readers will have their own robust opinions on which are the more deserving contenders, so if you know of a top sit that's been egregiously overlooked, why not message our Instagram page hampsteadheathbenches with a photo and description and we'll post it on the account, most likes wins.